The Meaning

Poetic and Spiritual Reflections

With an essay on Poetry and Spiritual Experience

T0159380

The Meaning

Poetic and Spiritual Reflections

With an essay on Poetry and Spiritual Experience

Steve Taylor

BOOKS

Winchester, UK
Washington, USA

First published by O-Books, 2012
O-Books is an imprint of John Hunt Publishing Ltd., Laurel House, Station Approach,
Alresford, Hants, SO24 9JH, UK
office1@o-books.net
www.o-books.com

For distributor details and how to order please visit the 'Ordering' section on our website.

Text copyright: Steve Taylor 2011

ISBN: 978 1 78099 303 4

A CIP catalogue record for this book is available from the British Library.

Design: Stuart Davies

Printed and bound by CPI Group (UK) Ltd, Croydon, CR0 4YY, UK

We operate a distinctive and ethical publishing philosophy in all
areas of our business, from our global network of authors to
production and worldwide distribution.

CONTENTS

The Trick

The trick is to trust yourself
not to try to trap your prey
or seduce your lover

If you feel frustrated
the animal will scent your anxiety
and veer away
your lover will sense your desperation
and spurn you

Your soul is delicate
you can't shake and squeeze her
or scrape her sides
for a few last crumbs of insight

She needs time to collect herself
to gather her dissipated power
Too much force will break the mould
of invisible patterns and potentials
which give birth to beauty

She may seem barren now
but she's not dead, only sleeping
New life is slowly seeping through
from that deep underground source
making her moist and rich again

until she's ready to release
strange new joys

Your soul has never let you down
and never will
as long as you are patient
as long as you are still.

The Meaning

You can't explain the meaning
Reduce it to thought or confine it to words
Break it down to basic building blocks
Or trace it back to an origin.

But when you see the meaning, you know it.
Just when you've forgotten it existed
You're driving along the motorway
and turn your head to the side
As if someone's tapped your shoulder
And it's there, stretched across the evening sky
Filling the spaces between the clouds.

You open the door to empty the bin
And it's there, rustling with the wind through the
    trees
Stroking your face softly like a lover.
You tilt your head back to catch the rain
And it's there, falling with the infinite silver points
Bringing down benevolence from the sky.

Your eyes spring open in the middle of the night
As if there's an intruder, an unfamiliar noise
And it's there - in the dense, rich darkness that fills
    the room
And the glow of unconscious communion
    that envelopes you and your lover.

The most familiar forgotten place
Your home from a previous lifetime
A mother's soothing presence
And her warm enfolding arms.

Forget the Past

Forget the past
It's just a dream you keep alive by dreaming
A bubble that wants to hit the ground and burst
But which you keep afloat by thinking.

The past is only a tail
You keep dragging behind you
Collecting dust and dirt
Until it's so heavy with bitterness and regret
It stops you moving forward.

You don't have to sit there and watch
While the scenes of your past play back
The tragi-comedy of your life
Simmering with hurt and envy
Shuddering with embarrassment
Stabbing yourself with pangs of regret.

There is no past
There are only memories of events
And every memory is refracted through
A hall of mental mirrors
Until whatever once was true
Dissipates and disappears
Like vapour trails fading in the sky.

So cut the tail, and cut the tale
Turn the mental projector off
Don't strain your eyes trying to see through the fog
When the panorama of the present stretches
Clear and bright around you.

The Secrets

You can't grasp at the secrets
Prise them from the earth
Or pluck them from the air.
The harder you try to hold them
The more they lose their form
Until they leak away.

You can grind matter down to the tiniest grains
Until it collapses into nothing
But its essence will always elude you.
You can pin nature down and torture her
But she'll never tell you what she knows.

You can't use force, or even effort
You can only create the right conditions
Reverse the beam of your attention
And make a sacred space inside.

Let your mind become as empty as a cloudless sky
And as calm as the surface of a lake
Until your depths are rich with stillness
And the channel is wide and clear enough
For the secrets to flow through
And reveal themselves to you.

The Standing Stones at Carnac

The earth was once alive
These sun-baked fields -
Now dotted with tents and caravans
And full of jostling tourists
With children complaining, 'Why do we have to look
at stones?' -
Were once a sacred site
Shimmering with strange energies
And hidden portals to higher worlds.

What's left are these giant jagged blocks
Tilting haphazardly over the hills
Like the lines of an ancient script
Which has never been deciphered
Gravestones of long-forgotten meaning.

They may seem empty, dead or dumb
Just because we can't connect
Can't enter their endless spacious depths
Or hear their soft and low vibrations
That's why we wander through these tourist streets
Searching for distractions and pleasures
To numb the pain of separation.

The stones aren't dead, just hibernating
Waiting for the world to turn
They're still attuned to the stars
Still collecting cosmic energy.

There's no one here to receive it, but they don't care
They'll keep staring straight ahead, impassively
Like wise old men, watching
As this mad wave falls and ebbs away
And five thousand years from now they'll still be
    here
When the caravans are ancient relics
Of a barbaric prehistoric age
And the earth will be sacred again.

Moments without Thought

A moment without thought
And the background noise ceases
And I can suddenly hear
The silence between sounds
The silence beneath sound
From which all sounds emerge
Like waves from the sea.

A moment without thought
And the fog disperses
And the world is filled
With translucent light
New dimensions of detail
And sharpness and colour and depth.

A moment without thought
And these suburban streets
Are a pristine new world
Like a garden glistening with dew
The morning after creation
As if a husk of familiarity
(The accumulated dust of a million automatic
        perceptions)
Has cracked and fallen away
Leaving naked primal isness.

A moment without thought
And I'm no longer standing separate
No longer an island but part of the sea
No longer a static centre
But part of the flowing stream.

A moment without thought
And the train has stopped between stations
And there was never any motion, never any track
A moment like a wormhole
Infinitely expanding
Like stepping through a narrow gate
To find an endless open plain
The panorama of the present.

And this new world of no-thought
Is neither alien nor unfamiliar
But a place where benevolence blows through the air
And soft shimmering energy fills every space
And the sunlight is the translucent white light of
    spirit
The deepest, closest, warmest place
The ground where I am rooted.

The Universal Lottery (to my Children)

Your eyes staring wide with wonder
At a million mundane miracles
'Who would have thought it?' they seem to say.
'Countless strands of DNA
Billions of potential people
And me, the chosen one,
Plucked out of oblivion
Given form and life and freedom
To explore this glorious gleaming world.
I've won the universal lottery
And I'm going to savour every moment.'

A shining surging fountain
Undiluted unpolluted
From the source of life itself
Every impulse like a ray of light
Blazing to expression.

Facing every moment
Like a flower open to the sun
Embracing every new experience
Like a friend from your last life-time.

No wonder you're so carefree.
How could problems ever exist
in a world so real and beautiful?
How could shadows of worry ever fall
Across such incandescent is-ness?

I will be your guide
I will nurture and protect you
But I have nothing to teach you
I can only learn.

What You Need

You don't need anyone
to remind you that you exist
to tell you that you're important
to treat you with respect
to bolster your fragile self-esteem
and disappoint you when they don't.

You don't need daily doses of good news
to lift your mood when you feel glum.
You don't need compliments or presents
or flirtatious smiles across the room
to keep you happy with yourself
or hourly fixes of pleasure
to set your brain cells jingling
and frustrate you when they don't.

You don't need to surround yourself with luxury
to treat yourself to the best of everything -
metallic fridges and designer bags
the colours of the season, the car of the year -
to show others that you're special
and feel incomplete when you can't.

You don't need to cover up the silence
with the chatter of radio and TVs.
You don't need to fill the empty space
with jobs that don't need doing
or words that have no meaning
or tasks that have no purpose
except to fill the empty space.

You don't need to occupy your mind
with activities and distractions
to keep your attention outside yourself
and feel naked when you can't.

Don't listen to the voice inside your head
that tells you there's no time to rest
that you have to keep moving and striving
like a sadistic old sports coach
or the voice that tells you you're not good enough
that you'll never be happy and don't deserve love
like a psychotic Victorian teacher
or the voice that whispers 'what if?'
and makes you fear the future.

You only need to meet yourself
to let the discord within you fade away
and find the stillness underneath
the place where you're already whole
where there is no need to seek or strive
because there is no need.

The Awakening Earth

The summer evening sky
Blue blotting paper with a thousand colours blurring
Splintering sunlight behind the clouds
As sharp and clear as laser beams

I can sense the turning of the earth
The whole solar system drifting through space
Like a raft that set sail billions of years ago
And I can see that the sky is not solid or finite
That there are no boundaries
Between the sky and the universe
These fields and the universe
Me and the universe

This is the cosmos
Surrounding me, immersing me
The same space that stretches
Through endless solar systems and galaxies
Fills this evening sky
Infinite emptiness
Which isn't blankly indifferent
but somehow benign and radiant

And I sense that the earth is a being of itself
Whose body is molten rock
Whose neo-cortex is this surface of soil
And whose neurons are living beings

And like a particle collapsing into a wave
An island sinking into the sea
The illusion of autonomy fades away
There is no I anymore
Only this glorious sentient pearl
This ocean flowing through me
This ocean which is me.

The Beginning of the Universe

When two lovers come together
And two cells meet and merge
There's a miniature big bang
And a universe begins.

It may seem inconsequential
Two strangers seeking pleasure
A drunken fling or favour
A jaded housewife's weekly chore

But really they're two gods
Creating a new reality
An awesome responsibility
A world to nurture and oversee.

Gases solidify and atoms collect
Consciousness spreads through the radiant void
And slowly the universe takes form and shape
Expanding and slowly settling.

Every universe is an experiment
A new web of planets and galaxies
Weaving new patterns and possibilities
Creating new laws of nature.

Every universe is an adventure
A voyage through uncharted time and space
Tentative steps forward and trail-blazing paths
Colliding and intersecting.

And every universe is a mystery
Filled with hidden fissures and tunnels
Teeming with invisible energies
And infinite, dark potentials.

And almost as soon as the expansion halts
The slow movement of entropy begins
The connections weaken and the fragments spread
Until the whole organism crumbles and collapses.

A slow decay or a giant crunch
And again the stillness of the void.

When You Lose Yourself

When you find yourself wondering
how you're going to pass the time
and scramble for arrangements
to fill the uneasy emptiness

When you find yourself wishing you were someone
   else
and stare enviously at the pages of magazines
wishing for better or more

When you catch yourself feeling that something's not
   quite right
but can't pin down what it is
When solitude feels unnerving
as if the room is filled with restless ghosts

When you catch your mind clinging to future dreams
looking forward to holidays a little too much
or find yourself hungry for noise and crowds
craving for action or activity
to immerse yourself in and forget

It's only a sign that you've lost touch with yourself
that there's a fog of worries and responsibilities
whirling through your mind
standing between you and the warmth and light
the spacious radiance of being.

It's only a sign that you've pushed yourself so hard
that you've dried up like a river in summer
and can't meet up with the ocean.

You don't need to do anything
You need to do nothing
to lift yourself out of the noise and stress
until the fog has cleared
and your being has settled to stillness
and the connection forms itself again.

I Am One of the Free

After centuries of darkness
I am in the light
After centuries in prison
I have been released.

I am one of the free
The end of a long line of slaves
Millworkers and miners
Strangers to the daylight
Sweating in the stale air
Deafened by the rattle of looms
Lungs filling up with cotton dust
Shaking each other to stay awake
(Because if they fell asleep they never woke up)
and shadows that stalked the underworld
suffocating slowly as they clawed the seams
in a darkness that sweltered with danger.

And before them, peasants and serfs
Shivering and starving through winter
Stooped over ploughs and scythes
Chained to patches of their masters' soil
Through endless stagnant centuries
Rounded up like cattle by lords and kings
To fight for scraps of land
Leaving their fields and families to rot.

Generations haunted by disease and death
Traumatised by fear and loss
Broken parents burying children
Orphaned children numbed and scarred
Left defenceless against a brutal world.

A whole world of possibility
Shrunk to a tiny dark circle of hell
Souls like rivers, deep and rich
Shrivelled to muddy pools.

Freedom isn't always easy
Too many choices can confuse you
Too much open space can make you feel exposed
Like soldiers at the end of a war
Unnerved by silence and stillness
You might feel guilty, that you don't deserve your
    freedom.

But what can we do but be grateful to them
For struggling through those centuries
To prise open this window of light?
And we can grow to deserve it by using it.

We owe it to them not to waste it
To never take it for granted
And always appreciate the fresh air and light
And the freedom to be, instead of just to do
To stop and look and contemplate
And most of all, the freedom to become

To explore the depths that were closed to them
To release the potential that was dammed inside
    them
And let ourselves flow as fast and as far as we can
And try to illuminate the darkness
That still fills the lives of others.

What is Missing

You've spent your whole life trying to complete yourself
but nothing has ever filled your sense of lack.
The craziest adventures, the most ecstatic love,
the most prized possessions, the most satisfying success -
nothing could alleviate your gnawing discontent.

There were times when your life seemed perfect,
with all ambitions satisfied and all problems solved -
and you told yourself, "That's it! I'm here! I've found
happiness at last!"

Then you'd wake up the next morning and it was back -
that familiar grasping feeling, that sense of "It's not
enough!"
like a background hum, a high-pitched screech of
hollowness.

But there is nothing missing from your life -
you are what is missing, from the vast, deep oneness of
being.
The lack you feel is your own separation.

A fragment is always broken, no matter what you add to it,
until you bring it back into union.

There is no hole inside you -
the whole is around you

waiting to embrace you
and dissolve your emptiness away.

The Wild Wind

The air turns to waves
Crashing and spraying against my face
Garden fences rattle
The limbs of trees flail
Dust tornadoes swirl
Through ancient pipes and chimneys

The earth's primeval roar
Scatters the clouds
Like white stampeding bulls
Over the sky's dark plain.

The Earth is breathing –
Ecstatic heavy breathing –
Reminding us she's still alive.

A World that Moves too Fast to Map

I went snorkelling once
And found a strange new planet under the sea
A new spectrum of colours
A new geometry of shapes
A new taxonomy of life forms
I was transfixed, exhilarated
I couldn't lift my head above the water for hours.

And now, above me, there's another new world
A sky more beautiful than any landscape I've ever
    seen.

Foaming continents of white
Tectonic plates shifting through millennia every
    second
Creating jagged new countries
And smooth still seas
Of unearthly perfect blue.
Ethereal streaks and curling strands
Disembodied sealess waves
Ghost-clouds arched to heaven.

And there, towards the horizon
Golden-framed granite blocks
Awesome and forbidding
With the sun sinking behind them.

And there....but no
The scene has already changed
The waves have dissipated
A foaming grey mist has swallowed the still blue
    lakes
I've lost the vision I wanted to describe.

This is a world that moves too fast to map
If you stand still you miss it.
You have to latch on to it
And swim with its flow.

The Festive Season

Late night shoppers buried by bags
Pavements strewn with broken glass
Office workers stumbling
with loosened ties and stained white shirts
Buses heaving and taxis circling
Sickly sweet alcoholic fumes
Swilling through the freezing air -
The festive season is here again.

I spent one New Year's Eve with a sociologist -
When the drinkers started counting down to midnight
He folded his arms and smiled with scorn.
'It doesn't mean anything - it's just a social construct,'
He shouted as the New Year exploded around us.
He may have been miserable but he was right.

There are no sacred days
There is only the spinning of the earth
Towards the sun and away again
Warming its face before the fire
Then turning again to the cold black space.

The year has no end or beginning
There is only the floating of the earth
Tilting through the seasons like a yacht at sea
Circling a course laid down by gravity.

Every day is sacred
Every moment of this journey
Every spin and tilt and curve
Every forward flow through space
And I will celebrate them all.

We Grow Together
(For Pam)

Love doesn't have to grow stale and old -
the longer we live together
the more we grow together
like branches intertwining
as they stretch towards the sun.

Who would have thought it, after all this time?
The air is still as fresh as spring
brushing the sides of our souls.
The soil is still rich and dark
crumbling around our roots.

Relationships can wither to a sad slow death
but not while two souls are still renewing,
conceiving new selves and reshaping the old.
Why should we stagger to a tired end
when there's so much more to explore?

There can't be entropy while there's evolution
there can't be decay while there's still growth
and we'll keep growing while we're still connected
like two clouds that float together
slowly merging until there's just one.

The Alchemy of Attention

When a mist of multiplying thoughts fills your mind
Associations spinning endlessly
Images jostling and memories whirling
Free-falling through your inner space
You can always bring yourself back to now.

This morning, making breakfast for the kids
I catch myself daydreaming and with a gentle mental
    nudge
Remind myself of where I am
And straight away the kitchen clutter turns to
    spacious presence
A mosaic of sunlit squares across the floor
Fading and brightening with the passing clouds
The metal rims of stools firing sparks
Steam-curls floating over cups
Reflecting silver spoons
The perfect stillness of spilt coffee grains
The gaudy yellow and blue of detergent bottles
And the window smudges exposed by sun -

Everything perfectly still and real
Everything perfectly itself.

Attention is an alchemy
That turns dullness to beauty
And anxiety to ease.

The Force

Four o'clock in the morning
pacing about the room
trying to coax our baby back to sleep
I look over to the window -
a square of pure primeval darkness
between the half drawn curtains
millions of years old
millions of miles deep
a pocket of the universe
a tunnel into space
black, cold and silent
but alive.

The force flows through the window
thick and viscous
but at the same time subtle and vapour thin
enveloping and entering me
like smoke, foaming through my body
slow and heavy, merging and becoming me.

Inside me there's only darkness
awesome and immense, almost frightening
but glowing with warm benevolence.

Making Time

Always struggling to make some time
To prise apart my duties
And claim a little space for myself
To fill with achievement and activity.

But why should I rush?
There is no shortage of time
I am not sandwiched between birth and death
The gates have dissolved away
And there's an endless open space.
This is only a phase
Not the entire journey.

There is no need to regret
Choices you have made
Opportunities you didn't take.
There will be time
To take other paths
And rectify mistakes.

Birth and death are only demarcations
Lines that we step over
Not walls that hem us in.

There will always be time.

Slow Down

The world keeps speeding up, moving much too fast -
that's why it's full of chaos
that's why it's heading for catastrophe.

You're being carried along by the momentum
and it's intoxicating, like a fairground ride.
But your adrenaline's already running dry
your limbs are stiffening from tension
and soon you'll start to lose your balance.
Your vision is losing focus
the patterns that were once so clear are blurring.

Slow down - don't be so desperate to reach the future
that you ignore the world, and push the present
    away.
Treat each moment with respect
as a friend that deserves your attention.
Greet every new experience as a guest
who's welcome to be a part of your life.

Slow down, so that the world can stop and astound you
with shimmering is-ness and shining beauty. Slow
down, so that the cosmos can connect with you and
embrace and absorb you into its whole.

Speed brings agitation and fragmentation -
slow down, and see how they gently fade away,

replaced by the ease and wholeness of slowness.

Slow down, and see how the future fades from view,
   like a mirage
and how the present arises, as clear and fresh as
   dawn.

Whenever you think

Whenever you think you're something
Remember that you are nothing.

Whenever you're full of your own success
And people applaud and compliment you
And you're proud of your achievements
Remember that you are nothing.

Whenever you think that you've arrived
Remember that this is a journey
With no destination, or even stations.
Whenever you think you're the centre of the world
Remember this is only the circumference
And the world will turn without you.

Whenever you think you have the answers
Remember that questions are never fixed
But always flowing and reforming.
Whenever you think you're going somewhere
Remember there is never anywhere but here.

And then
When you know that you are nothing
When you know that you are nowhere
Remember that you are everything
Remember that you are everywhere
Remember that you are.

The Scarecrow Trees

The scarecrow trees
Clawing the darkness
Against the curve of the hills
Are speaking an ancient language
A vibration so slow and deep
Words that take hundreds of years to voice
Stretched across the centuries
Like an infinite string
The echo of a cosmic accident
From the beginning of the universe.

I am an intruder
But as I walk amongst them
An ancient part of me
Deeper than my mind
Older than my body
Catches the vibration and stirs to life
Like a refugee who hears his native tongue.

The River inside me

There is a river inside me
Rippling with effervescent life
Gently pulsating with waves of bliss.

Sometimes I'm pulled away to the plateau
And join the crowds jostling for space and time
I lose myself amongst the melee
Like a plant so entangled
It can't trace its roots back to the ground.
Sometimes I'm swept away by whirls of thought
Cascades of images and scenarios
That cloud the present until it almost disappears.

But the thread is never broken
And when the storm fades away and stillness returns
I sink back gently and let the river immerse me again.

And sometimes when my mind is silent
My whole being becomes translucent
The barriers dissolve
This river swells and spills
Until I overflow with ecstasy
And return to the Source.

The River of Life

It's not enough to live from day to day
Keeping yourself warm, well-fed and safe
Satisfying desires, chasing after fun
Hiding from the strange and dangerous
Dazed with distractions and daydreams.

Life shouldn't be a tepid pond
But a river flowing fast and furious
Full of struggles and adventures
That open up new depths
And awaken higher selves.

The same river that has brought you here
Through billions of years of unfolding
An ever-widening stream, from a trickle to a torrent -
Not to rest, but to keep cutting through
Until your being is ocean deep and wide.

Outside the Human World

Sometimes we have to step outside the human world
outside the tangled webs of relationships
the hanging threads of unfinished tasks
the deadlines that press into the present
the crowded confines of human time
the scramble for status and success
and the mad media pressure to consume.

Sometimes we have to step into the non-human world
into the timeless spacious stillness of the landscape
where it's such a relief to realise
that our world is just one, amongst millions of others -
just a crazy sideshow, rather than centre stage.

The cold primeval worlds of rocks and mountains
the slow and stately worlds of trees
the frenetic worlds of insects
and infinite mysterious underwater worlds -
every species carves out its own reality
with its own configuration of consciousness,
too murkily strange and secret for us to conceive of.
A shared psychic space binds each species together so
    tightly
that they scarcely seem aware of us.

But all of these other worlds intersect and interconnect
nourishing, not conflicting, with their difference.

It's only the human world that separates itself, and holds
    the rest to ransom
believing we can survive alone.

And if it should come to pass, that we suffocate in our
    separateness
and die from disconnection
the other worlds will register a tremor faraway
and no matter how badly damaged they are -
they will recover, and continue, nonchalant.

The Night is Alive

I wake up to the diluted darkness
Grey geometric streets
Only a few stars strong enough
To penetrate the orange streetlight glow.

But the night is alive
The space from the ground to the sky
Is filled with a crackling electric haze
Particles spinning and clashing
As they weave in and out of existence.

The hissing of cosmic radiance
From the first millisecond of creation
And encompassing every moment since.
Every dispersed atom, swimming across this endless
	sea,
Singing their original oneness.

The Intruder

Who is this intruder?
This black shadow spreading across the bright open
     space
this uninvited guest
poisoning the atmosphere with pride
chattering and smiling smugly
curving the currents of air
sucking attention towards itself
like a black hole.

There should be something pure and full here
a shimmering golden cloud
the still surface of a lake
some unknown element
lighter than gas, heavier than air
glowing with a heat that never burns
intensely bright but never blinding.

It's still there - I can sense it.
Trapped inside the room,
I can hear it outside.
A pure blue sky covered by cloud.

But the shadow is stalking
standing astride
making distinctions
defining a space

demarcating his territory
assuming an identity
occupying emptiness.

The Structure Dissolves

I don't know whether this is desperation or elation
There's only a gentle push between the two
The slightest breeze could sway me to either side
But somehow it doesn't matter
It's just the same landscape through a different lens.

A structure which seemed so sturdy
So deep-rooted I didn't even realise it was there
A house I hardly ever set foot outside
And started to think was the whole world
Is so fragile that it's about to dissolve.

Just a certain frequency
A certain pitch of stress and turmoil
And the ego edifice crumbles
Leaving nothing behind
A trail of dissipating smoke.

I don't know what's behind it
What will emerge in its place
But something vast and subtle
A pressure, gentle but unstoppable
Is pushing through.

All I have to do is trust it
To let myself be blanked out
To let this island be submerged
By the mighty ocean.

A Spring Day

It's one of those spring days
when gardens are flashing and sparkling
like a slow-motion firework display
and streets are scattered with blossom
as if a wedding party has just passed by
and the whole world seems ready to celebrate.

It's one of those spring days
when the wind blows with an urgency
carrying messages from tree to tree
while the sunlight glints expectantly
and clouds rush across the sky
as if they all know a miracle is imminent.

It's one of those spring days
when the dark dusty corners of my being
are flushed with freshness and life again
and the certainty arises, from a deep forgotten place,
that all is well, and all will be well, always.

Sleeping Baby (Finally)

It takes so long to get him to sleep
but when he finally goes
he falls so far
into silent stillness.

I peer between the curtains
at the radiant blackness between the stars
and I can hear subtle vibrations of harmony
echoing from the depths of the universe.

And that's where he is
floating through the infinite universe
of his own being
stars shining inside him
the sea gently swelling
with slow serene waves
inside him.

The End of Desire

If what you want is endless pleasure, wealth or fame
Then you will always want.
You will never reach a place of peace
You will never rest content
The tentacles of desire will always be grasping.

A few moments of respite
While you digest the experience
And then the same restless hunger
The gnawing incompleteness
Only a little more powerful and rarefied
Because your palette is a little more refined
And your sense of taste a little more dulled.

Desire is like a fertilised cell
That forever splits and multiplies
And never reaches a final form
Only disperses and dilutes your mind
And takes you even further away from the source.

You might think you've reached the end of desire
But then the mist clears
And you realise this peak is only a plateau
The bottom of an even higher peak.

The harder you search for happiness
Turning the world upside down
For a legendary treasure which was never there
The more you lose touch with the shining source
Of peace and joy inside you.

Don't desire anything
except the end of desire.

Afterword

Using Words to Go Beyond Words:
Poetry and Spiritual Experience

Poetry is the natural medium to communicate higher states of consciousness, or awakening experiences. Everyday language belongs to everyday consciousness; its structures are a reflection of those of normal consciousness itself. Since our normal state is to see ourselves as separate to the world, as beings 'in here' looking out at a world 'out there', the basic structure of the English language (and other European languages) is a subject/duality, an 'I' or 'you' acting on things which are separate to it. And since we have a strongly linear sense of time, and our thoughts are often focused on the past and the future, ordinary language is split into tenses, and is full of terms referring to the future and the past. This contrasts with the languages of many indigenous peoples, which don't have different tenses, and only have vague, general terms to cover notions of the past and future.

As a result, it's difficult to describe awakening experiences in ordinary language. It's like trying to catch water with a net. That's why some spiritual traditions only attempt to explain the experiences in negative terms, as in 'neti neti' (not this, not this) in the Upanishads. As the 16th century Jewish mystic, Isaac Luria, is believed to have told his disciples, 'I can hardly open my mouth to speak without feeling as though the sea bursts its dam and overflowed. How then shall I express what my soul has received?'

But poetry is a way of expressing the inexpressible. It isn't bound by the normal constraints of language. It doesn't have to convey meaning directly, but can just suggest it, through allusion, image and metaphor. It can take the conventional signs and symbols of language – designed to convey information – and convey something *more* than information with them: real, felt experience. In philosophical terms, it can be truly *intersubjective* – that is, it can create a real communication of being, an exchange of feeling. There is a Zen saying that 'The finger that points to the moon is not the moon.' But good poetry *can* be the moon.

Wordsworth defined poetry as 'the spontaneous overflow of powerful feelings.' When we have powerful feelings and experiences, there's often an impulse to 'frame' them in poetry. To capture experience in this way may seem wrong, a manifestation of the acquisitive impulse, like the desire to catch and collect butterflies. Surely we should just let our experience flow by, without holding on to it? But we need to frame intense experiences so that we can *re*collect them and relive them. Wordsworth also described the origin of poetry as 'emotion recollected in tranquillity,' and my guess is that for him poetry was an *aid* to recollection too, a way of rekindling his moments of serenity and awe.

It's useful beyond words – literally – for us to be able to return to these moments, particularly when the everyday world overwhelms us and we feel oppressed by anxieties. And of course, it's useful beyond words for us to pass on these experiences to others, so that readers can gain a taste of our spiritual experiences when *they* are oppressed by anxieties – or even when they're not. Spiritual poetry is sustenance for the soul, a reminder of higher realities when we're stranded amongst lower ones.

In this sense, poetry can be a 'transmitter' of spiritual experiences. Like the best composers or painters, a good poet can describe his or her experience so clearly that it's transmitted through to a receptive reader, who then experiences something of the same state. When I see paintings by Van Gogh or Turner, I experience something of the amazing intensity of their vision, just as when I listen to Gorecki's third symphony or Marvin Gaye's *What's Goin' On*, my soul stirs to the drama and power – and the sorrow and ecstasy – of the music. And in the case of spiritual poems, this means that spiritual experiences can be passed on to the reader. In my research, I have found that reading poetry or spiritual texts can be a significant (although admittedly not one of the *most* significant) trigger of both temporary spiritual experiences and permanent spiritual awakening. Reading poetry can therefore be seen as a type of spiritual practice – and indeed, it is considered as such in some monastic traditions, as in the traditional Catholic practice of 'contemplative reading' (*lectio divina*, literally 'divine reading') of passages from the Bible.

The Tradition of Spiritual Poetry

There is a long tradition of poets who were also mystics, and whose main poetic aim was to convey the insights and visions which came from their awakening experiences. In English literature, this tradition begins in the 17th century, with poets like Henry Vaughan and Thomas Traherne. Vaughan and Traherne were both Christian mystics whose poetry is pervaded with an awareness of the divine in the ordinary world, and a sense that 'heaven' is not a place beyond the earth but a condition *of* the world, which is always present but which our senses normally close us off to.

Although spirituality – particularly in relation to nature – was a common theme of the whole Romantic movement of the late 18th and early 19th centuries, Blake, Wordsworth and Shelley were the most overtly spiritual of the Romantics. Wordsworth has many beautiful passages in which he describes the presence of an all-pervading spiritual force in the world – for example, in *Tintern Abbey*, 'A motion and a spirit, that impels/All thinking things, all objects of all thought,/And rolls through all things.' This is clearly what the Upanishads refer to as *Brahman*, the 'invisible and subtle essence' which 'is the spirit of the whole universe.' Shelley was aware of it too, describing it in 'Hymn to Intellectual Beauty' as 'Spirit of beauty' and 'The awful shadow of some unseen Power/[which] Floats though unseen among us.'

In the 19th century, the tradition was continued most explicitly by Christian mystics such as Gerald Manley Hopkins and Francis Thompson. The poet laureate – and probably the most popular poet of the Victorian era - Alfred Lord Tennyson was very familiar with awakening experiences too, such as when he described a form of mantra meditation, repeating his own name until his 'individuality itself seemed to dissolve and fade away into boundless being.'

More recently, the poetic spiritual tradition was carried forward by D.H. Lawrence, Ted Hughes, Kathleen Raine and R.S. Thomas (another Christian mystic). Although very different, Lawrence and Hughes were both mystics who didn't exist in ego-separateness but were able to enter into the being of other human beings, animals, plants and the Earth itself. Hughes' mysticism was much less intense than Lawrence's, but he shared the latter's ability to 'see into the life of things' (in Wordsworth's phrase). The Welsh poet and clergyman R.S. Thomas had a reputation for austerity and gloom, but his poems are pervaded with the same sense of the divine as Thomas Traherne's, even if the divine is not as apparent in the everyday world. For example, in his poem 'Blackbird':

...........Do not despair
at the stars' distance. Listening
to blackbird music is
to bridge in a moment chasms
of space-time, is to know
that beyond the silence

which terrified Pascal
there is a presence whose language
is not our language...

And this is just in English literature. France has its own poet-mystics, such as Lamartine and Rimbaud. Germany has many more, including Goethe, Holderlin and Novalis. America has a similarly rich tradition – only with less overtly religious overtones – with spiritual poets such as Walt Whitman, Emily Dickinson, Thoreau and Emerson, and in modern times, nature-mystics such as Mary Oliver and Wendell Berry.

All of these poets were – or are – very spiritually developed individuals who had frequent awakening experiences, which were the mainspring of their poetry. Some of them were tortured by the seeming inaccessibility of awakening experiences, and the gulf between the world of meaning and harmony they revealed and the seeming emptiness and bleakness of the world of everyday consciousness. This is Shelley's complaint in 'Hymn to Intellectual Beauty.' As he laments to the 'Spirit of Beauty': 'Why dost thou pass away and leave our state/ This dim vast vale of tears, vacant and desolate?'

Rimbaud was tortured by this gulf too. After experiencing higher states of consciousness which gave him a 'vision of purity' he found the shadowy, limited reality of ordinary consciousness impossible to endure. He describes being 'brought back down to earth, with a duty to find and a gnarled reality to embrace!' This frustration may have been one of the reasons why, at the age of just 19, he abandoned his attempts to become a visionary and, at the same time, abandoned poetry. Other poets didn't experience this frustration though, because a higher state of consciousness was normal to them. They didn't just have spiritual experiences, but existed in a permanently spiritual state. This was true of my D.H. Lawrence and Walt Whitman, for example, my own two favourites.

People are sometimes surprised when I refer to Lawrence as a mystic, partly because of his popular reputation as a sexual liberator, and also because there are so many other facets to him: working class novelist, playwright, travel writer, anthropologist, painter, and so on. And it's true that Lawrence doesn't have many of the outward signs of spirituality – little knowledge of eastern spiritual traditions or spiritual practices, and seemingly little of the serenity and detachment which 'enlightened' individuals display. But this is also partly because his mystical vision is conveyed most fully through his poems, which are largely forgotten next to his novels. Lawrence was amazingly prolific in his short life (he died at the age of 44) and wrote close to 1000 poems, in addition to over 40 books.

Admittedly, a lot of Lawrence's poetry isn't particularly good. Many of his earlier poems seem awkward, as if he was struggling with a form he wasn't suited to. He only found his true poetic voice in the last few years of his life, once he abandoned conventional verse forms and let his insights express themselves spontaneously, letting content dictate form. His natural wakefulness also intensified towards the end of his life, particularly during his final few months, as he was dying of tuberculosis. Despite their occasional bitterness at the madness of human beings, his final poems – published after his death as *More Pansies* and *Last Poems* – are the most profound and spiritual works he wrote, filled with an awareness of spiritual radiance pouring through the world, and a sense of deep serenity. Lawrence sees God – or gods – everywhere around him. It is the presence of the gods which 'makes the air so still and lovely to me…And I fall asleep with the gods.' He feels a deep peace inside him which he describes as 'Like a cat asleep on a chair/ at peace, in peace / feeling the presence of the living God.'

And most movingly of all, Lawrence greeted his imminent death with equanimity, and even joy. Like all mystics, he sensed that the death of the body is not the end of life. He describes death as 'the great adventure' in which 'the winds of the afterwards kiss us into the blossom of manhood…after the painful, painful experience of dying/ there comes an after-gladness, a strange joy.'

Whitman never struggled with his poetry as Lawrence did. His poetic voice was authentic and assured from the beginning. His awakened state seems to have been intense from the beginning too. For me, Whitman's *Leaves of Grass* is as great a spiritual text as *The Upanishads*. Both books are so bright with spiritual radiance that reading them is like staring straight at the sun – a dazzling and sometimes dizzying experience. I can't read either them without being filled with euphoria and reassurance, sensing that they're describing the fundamental reality of the universe, in all its harmony and overpowering meaning.

In fact, it's possible to say that in some ways *Leaves of Grass* is even greater than *The Upanishads*. Whereas the latter are a little detached, with no real connection to the everyday human world, Whitman depicts the radiance of *Brahman* pouring into all aspects of human life, from the messiest and most mundane to the most exalted. *The Upanishads* tell us that all is *Brahman*, that we are one with the universe, and that the soul is deathless, but Whitman *shows* it. Spirit doesn't just shine through space and through nature, but through the craftsmen, soldiers and sailors who Whitman meets, through sex and friendship, and even through warfare, illness and death. As Whitman describes it himself:

> I see something of God each hour of the twenty-four,
> and each moment then,
> In the faces of the men and women I see God, and in
> my own face in the glass...

It was because of this all-embracing spirituality that Richard M. Bucke – author of *Cosmic Consciousness* – described Whitman as the 'highest instance of cosmic consciousness.' Knowing Whitman personally, Bucke noted that Whitman had completely integrated his 'enlightenment' into his life, rather than allowing it to 'tyrannize over the rest.' It wasn't a distinct part of his

personality, which he kept separate from his job or relationships, but one which illuminated every aspect of his life
and his personality. He didn't meditate for days on end, or
go to live in a monastery or forest; he carried his spirituality with him into the everyday world.

The Guru as Poet

In a permanently awakened state, poetry flows naturally
and easily. There is no struggle for inspiration. The
heaviness and narrowness of ordinary consciousness
blocks creativity – its automaticity of perception, its
dullness of feeling and its separateness. It's when they're
trapped in this mode of consciousness that writers
experience 'writers' block.' In this mode, the ego is closed
off to everything apart from its own desires and thoughts;
it struggles to have a relationship with anything beyond
itself. In the awakened state, however, perception is always
fresh and intense, and there's a constant flow of new
energies and potentials. The awakened self experiences no
separation, so the world is constantly entering into it and it
into the world. As a result, in Wordsworth's phrase, there is
a constant 'overflow of powerful feelings.'

It's this 'open' state which gives rise both to spiritual
experience and to poetry. Poets and mystics are people with
very labile self-boundaries, who aren't trapped inside the
cramped shell of the ego. It doesn't mean that all poets are
mystics, or that all mystics are poets, but it means that they
often overlap.

This is why the connection between poetry and spirituality works the other way around too. In the same way that many poets were also mystics, a high proportion of people best known as mystics – or enlightened beings or spiritual teachers – were also poets. Many of the greatest spiritual figures in human history have chosen poetry as their main (if not their only) medium of expression. In the Sufi tradition, there are mystic-poets such as Rumi, Attar and Kabir, while the Buddhist tradition has enlightened poets such as Milarepa, Basho and Hakuin. In the Hindu tradition, several more recent spiritual teachers have been prolific poets, including Sri Aurobindo, Vivekananda – and most recently – Sri Chimnoy.

And of course, many of the world's great spiritual texts are written in a poetic form too. Could there be any poetry more majestic than *The Upanishads* or the *Bhagavad-Gita*? Or any text more beautifully suggestive and allusive than the *Tao Te Ching*? Just as Whitman and Lawrence were great mystics, the authors of The Upanishads were great poets. Their language was precise and stately, never a word wasted or misplaced, and they knew the perfect images and metaphors to convey meaning - for example, 'Like a tree everlasting he [*Brahman*] stands in the centre of the heaven, and his radiance illumines all creation' (Svetasvatara Upanishad), or 'Even as a spider sends forth and draws in its thread, even as plants arise from the earth and hairs from the body of man, even so the whole creation arises from the Eternal' (Mundaka Upanishad).

It doesn't matter whether these texts were consciously

written as poetry – when awakened people express themselves, it often *becomes* poetry. In this sense, as well as being the natural medium to communicate spiritual experience, poetry is its natural *expression*. It's the natural *out-breath* of spiritual experience, and it emerges from it as naturally as vegetation emerges from the soil. As a result, it's not surprising that the distinction between poets and mystics is so blurred.

My own Poetical Journey

I started writing poetry at the age of 16. I still vividly remember the summer evening when I wrote my first ever poems. I stayed up late, after my parents had gone to bed, and lay on the floor in my room, writing feverishly into the back of one of my school exercise books. I felt like a river flowing, as if something had broken open inside me. A few months before, I had emerged from a carefree childhood into the paralysing self-consciousness of adolescence, and the poems were mostly the expression of my confusion and unease.

One of my favourite poems at that time was Shelley's 'The Mask of Anarchy.' I was also a big fan of The Doors, and an admirer of Jim Morrison's impressionistic, carefully wrought early lyrics, like 'The Crystal Ship,' 'Soul Kitchen' and 'My Eyes Have Seen you.' I liked Shelley's and Morrison's anti-authoritarian stance, and for a while I wrote silly revolutionary poems, such as one beginning 'We are all imprisoned in the cage of law.'

Shortly after that, we read 'Dover Beach' by Matthew Arnold in my A level English class, which touched me deeply. I still think it's a wonderful poem, as an expression of the insecurity of the Victorian age, when the 'Sea of faith' was retreating and the certainty and comfort of religion slipping away. I quickly bought a volume of Arnold's poetry and identified with his vulnerability and existential anxiety. I still occasionally quote the lines from his poem 'To Marguerite' as a description of 'ego-isolation':

Yes: in the sea of life en'isled
With echoing straits between us thrown
Dotting the shoreless watery wild,
We mortal millions live *alone.*

At university I studied English and American Literature, and although I read a lot of great books, I found the course very disappointing. I always felt there was a great gulf between literary criticism and literature itself. I saw them as expressions of different parts of the human mind which didn't belong together. Literary criticism was like analysing the dots in a blown up photograph, and missing the meaning of the photograph as a whole. I also felt it was arrogant of my professors to take other people's poems and novels and presume to interpret them as if they had written them themselves. If any of them had been writers or poets themselves I would have had more respect for them. In almost every other area, it's normal for pundits or 'experts' to be people who have a background in the field they're discussing. For example, almost all football pundits are retired players or managers, and business 'experts' are usually economists or businessmen themselves. But in the case of literary criticism, the 'experts' on artistic creations usually aren't creative themselves. As a result, I became very disenchanted with the course. I stopped going to lectures, and tried to make sure that my essays included digs at the enterprise of literary criticism.

During this time, and over the following few years, I carried on writing poetry, even though none of it was very good. In my early twenties, I went through a powerful mystical phase. I'd discovered *The Upanishads* and other spiritual texts, and also the spiritual music of Van Morrison. I was filled with a constant sense of exuberance and meaning. I felt that I had finally left depression and frustration behind and emerged as a new higher self, connected to something transcendent. My poetry reflected this too, moving away from gloom and self-pity to more spiritual themes, but I still wasn't happy with it. I had a couple of poems from that time published, but when I read them now, I find myself wincing slightly with embarrassment. Since I loved the Romantic poets so much, and spiritual mavericks like Whitman and Lawrence, I attempted to emulate their style, but in modern times that style just seems awkward and pretentious. For example, in my early twenties, I wrote a poem called 'Quiet and Serene is the Night' which began:

Quiet and serene is the night

Emptied of people and cars
The loud, distracting sounds of day
Have dissolved into rightful silence.

Now the only democratic curfew
Reigns within the streets
Now the restless city sleeps
Beneath a sheet of silence.

Throughout all these years, the problem was that I hadn't found my voice. I felt like I was trying to speak in a language I didn't know properly. I had the impulse, but not the right expression. My vocabulary seemed clumsy and I couldn't find the right rhythm, like a runner when he's out of the 'zone.' So eventually, I stopped writing poetry altogether. I didn't feel any sense of loss, since I was writing other things instead. Over ten or eleven years, I only wrote a handful of poems.

I never even thought about writing poetry again. So imagine my surprise when, in about 2006, shortly after our second baby Ted was born, the 'muse' descended on me again. I have absolutely no idea why – for some reason poems just seemed to form in my mind. The impulse came back to me. Perhaps it was because I was taking a break from writing prose. It was after the publication of *The Fall*, and before I had started to work on my next book, *Making Time*. I had been very focused on writing non-fiction for most of the last ten years. Before *The Fall* (which took me about four years to research and write) I had written *Out of*

Time and two other books which were never published. So perhaps my mind was empty and open to new creative energies. But the strange thing was that – again, for no obvious reason – I had acquired an authentic poetic voice. Whereas before I had always struggled, now the lines came easily. I didn't have to consciously strive for the right rhythm or the right phrases. They seemed to naturally form themselves. It was a bit like waking up in the morning and finding you can speak a foreign language. And ever since then, the voice has stayed with me, although there are long periods when it doesn't make itself heard.

I've learned not to force poems, or to worry if they don't come. (The poem 'The Trick' is partly about this.) I'm happy with the ones which have come through so far, and if there are no more, so be it. But there certainly is a connection between them and my spiritual state. As you will have realised, several of the poems are direct descriptions of my awakening experiences. Like most of us, I go through periods when I feel more 'spiritual' than others – periods when I feel strongly connected to a deeper part of my being, when I'm more aware of the beauty and is-ness of my surroundings, when I feel a constant sense of connection and meaning, and so on. Not surprisingly, those are the times when poems come most frequently – although I'm still aware that they also tend to come during the spaces between books.

I see these poems as part of the tradition of 'spiritual poetry' which I mentioned earlier (and as Keith Sagar kindly places them in his comment on the back of this book). I certainly don't consider myself the equal of poets like Wordsworth, Whitman or Lawrence – heaven forbid! But I certainly feel some kinship with them, and believe that my poems spring from the same source as theirs. And I hope that my poems have transmitted a degree of transcendence to you – the reader – and so helped you connect to that source as well.

BOOKS

O is a symbol of the world, of oneness and unity; this eye represents knowledge and insight. We publish titles on general spirituality and living a spiritual life. We aim to inform and help you on your own journey in this life.

Visit our website: http://www.o-books.com

Find us on Facebook:
https://www.facebook.com/OBooks

Follow us on Twitter: @obooks